AF594412

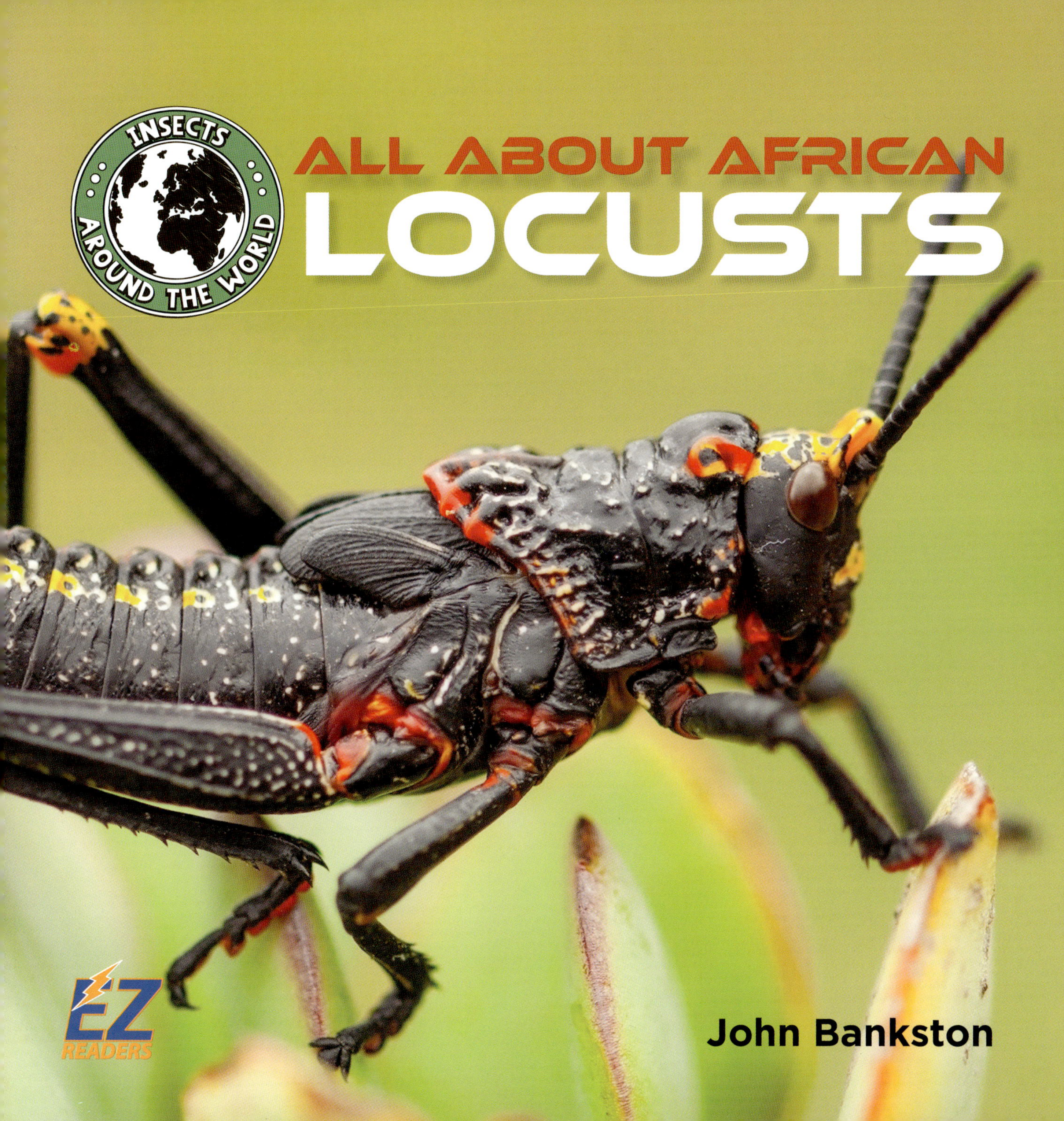
INSECTS
AROUND THE WORLD
ALL ABOUT AFRICAN
LOCUSTS
EZ READERS
John Bankston

Creating Young Nonfiction Readers

EZ Readers lets children delve into nonfiction at beginning reading levels. Young readers are introduced to new concepts, facts, ideas, and vocabulary.

Tips for Reading Nonfiction with Beginning Readers

Talk about Nonfiction
Begin by explaining that nonfiction books give us information that is true. The book will be organized around a specific topic or idea, and we may learn new facts through reading.

Look at the Parts
Most nonfiction books have helpful features. Our *EZ Readers* include a Contents page, an index, and color photographs. Share the purpose of these features with your reader.

Contents
Located at the front of a book, the Contents displays a list of the big ideas within the book and where to find them.

Index
An index is an alphabetical list of topics and the page numbers where they are found.

Glossary
Located at the back of the book, a glossary contains key words/phrases that are related to the topic.

Photos/Charts
A lot of information can be found by "reading" the charts and photos found within nonfiction text. Help your reader learn more about the different ways information can be displayed.

With a little help and guidance about reading nonfiction, you can feel good about introducing a young reader to the world of *EZ Readers* nonfiction books.

Mitchell Lane
PUBLISHERS

2001 SW 31st Avenue
Hallandale, FL 33009
www.mitchelllane.com

First Edition, 2023.

Author: John Bankston
Designer: Ed Morgan
Editor: Morgan Brody

Names/credits:
Title: All About African African Locusts / by John Bankston
Description: Hallandale, FL :
Mitchell Lane Publishers, [2023]

Series: Insects Around the World
Library bound ISBN: 978-1-68020-758-3
eBook ISBN: 978-1-68020-769-9

EZ Readers is an imprint of Mitchell Lane Publishers

Photo credits: Shutterstock.com, freepik.com

CONTENTS

Locusts and grasshoppers are related. There is one big difference. Locusts can change **behavior**.

Locusts usually like to be alone. Sometimes they become **social**. These locusts form **swarms** that can stretch for hundreds of miles. There can be billions of locusts in a single swarm. These swarms are a huge problem.

Using the wind for speed and distance, swarms can travel 80 miles a day. Groups of swarms are called a plague. Plagues destroy crops. Many people in Africa have starved because of locusts. The worst locust plague in 70 years hit Kenya in 2020.

10

Locusts only live for a few months. They start life as an egg. It takes anywhere from two weeks to several months for eggs to hatch.

Baby locusts are called **nymphs**. Because they can't fly, they are also called hoppers. They shed their skin five times before becoming adults. Adults have wings.

When there is a lot of rain, locusts group together and form swarms. This makes them change color, shape, and behavior. **Solitary** nymphs match color to their surroundings and keep to themselves.

Swarming nymphs are black and orange or yellow. They become adults quickly. Adult solitary locusts are usually green. Swarming adults are black with bigger muscles.

A locust can be as small as half an inch but some are three inches long. They weigh 0.07 ounces or about two grams.

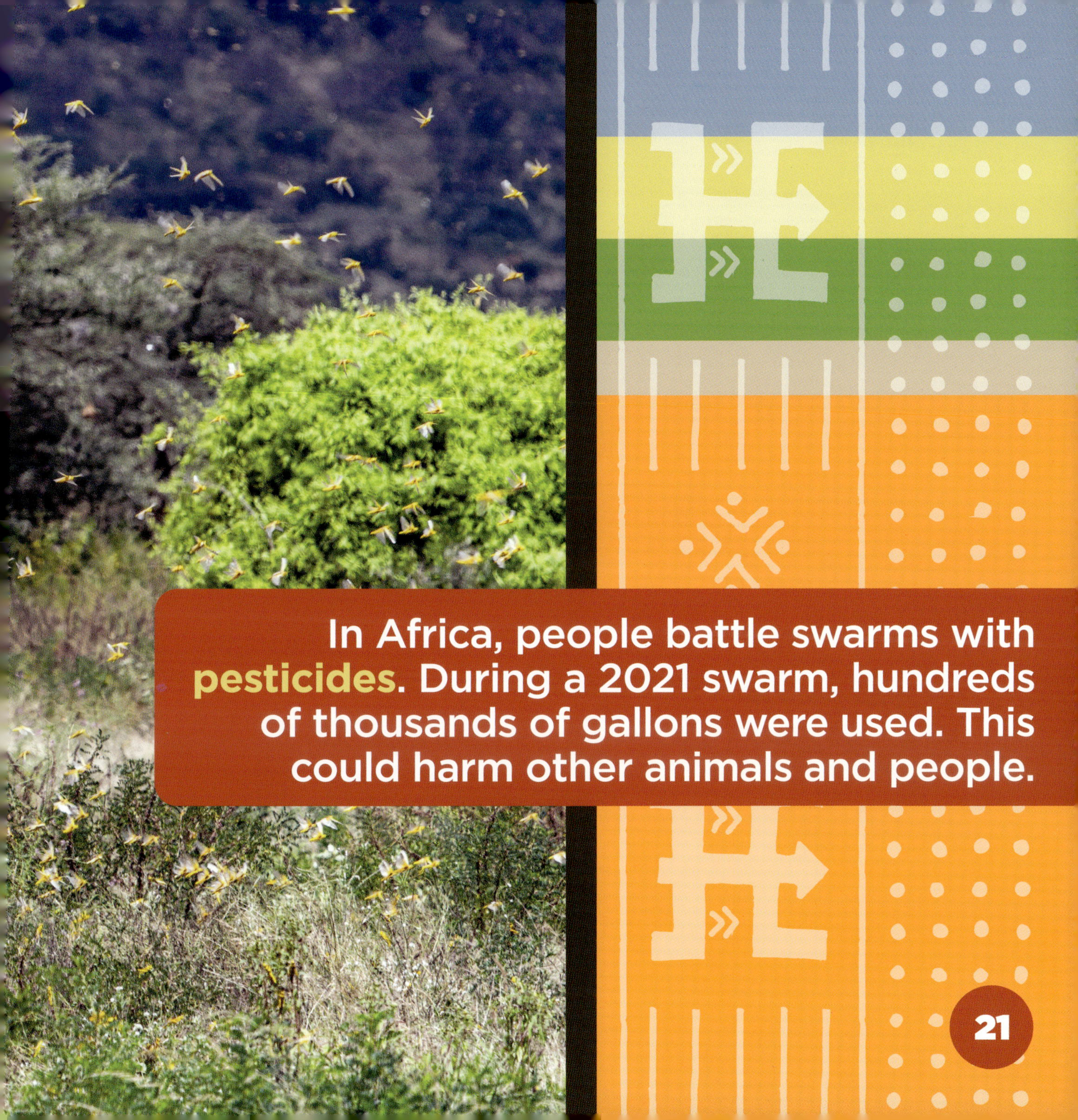

In Africa, people battle swarms with **pesticides**. During a 2021 swarm, hundreds of thousands of gallons were used. This could harm other animals and people.

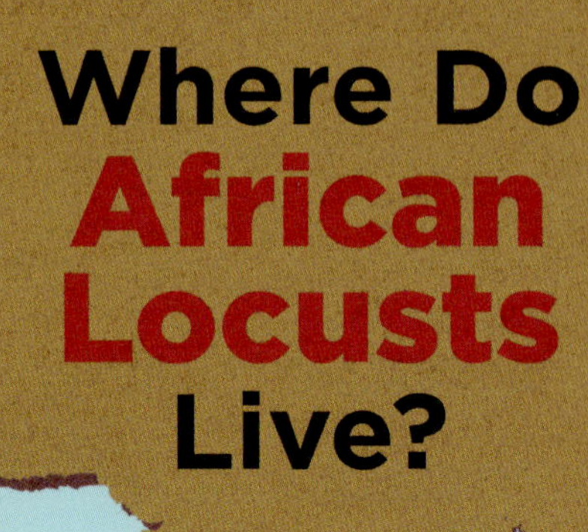

Where Do **African Locusts** Live?

Africa

Across Africa, there are four **species** of locusts. The desert locust lives in the drier northern region, especially Chad, Mali, Niger, Saudi Arabia, and Yemen. During swarms it can spread to 30 countries in Africa. The African **migratory** locust has the greatest range. The red locust mainly lives in Eastern Africa while the brown locust is found in South Africa and across the southern part of the continent.

INTERESTING FACTS

- In 1955, a locust swarm traveled from northwest Africa to England. In 1988, a swarm flew from the western coast of Africa to the Caribbean. It took the swarm just ten days to travel over 3,000 miles!
- A locust eats its body weight in food every day.
- A swarm covering one square mile can eat as much food as 40,000 people.
- Some think **climate** change is increasing the number of locust swarms. If there are more warm, wet days locusts are more likely to become social.
- Barbecued desert locust is a popular dish in Togo, a country in West Africa.

PARTS OF A LOCUST

Abdomen

The locust receives sounds through the ear which is on the first section of the **abdomen**.

Eyes

When a locust sees green, it gets excited. This is partly because of its two huge **compound** eyes. These eyes let it see over a large area.

Head

Has a pair of **antennae** or feelers used for smelling, compound eyes, a mouth, and jointed palps used for tasting food. Palps are jointed appendages connected to its head.

Thorax

The thorax is the middle section of the locust. It contains muscles for walking jumping and flying, and to which the wings and legs are attached. It also has a **sheath** covering called the pronotum.

The locust breathes through small holes along its thorax and abdomen. These are called spiracles. The locust is covered by three layers of skin called a cuticle. Tiny hairs cover the cuticle. These help it find out wind direction.

GLOSSARY

abdomen
Part of the body after the thorax containing the stomach and internal organs

antennae
Found on the insect's head and are used to detect smells

appendages
Smaller part of the body attached to a larger part

behavior
The way a creature acts, especially toward others

climate
Weather conditions over a long period of time

compound
Combination of several things

migratory
Moving from one place to another

nymph
Flightless stage between egg and adulthood

pesticides
Chemicals used to control insects or other "pests."

sheath
A protective covering

species
A group of very similar living creatures such as grasshoppers, crickets, and locusts

social
Comfortable in a group

solitary
Locusts that avoid other locusts. They behave as individuals

swarm
A large group of insects

FURTHER READING

Carmichael, L. E. *Locust Migration*. Parker, CO: Child's World, 2012.

Markle, Sandra. *Locusts: An Augmented Reality Experience*. Minneapolis, MN: Lerner, 2021.

ON THE INTERNET

"Locusts," National Geographic
https://www.nationalgeographic.com/animals/invertebrates/facts/locusts

Watch these videos of recent locust swarms in South Africa and Saudi Arabia
https://www.youtube.com/watch?v=QFI9A9zkON8
https://www.youtube.com/watch?v=DuRytoWqefE

INDEX